THIS STRANGE LAND

THIS STRANGE LAND

Shara McCallum

Alice James Books

FARMINGTON, MAINE

10 9 8 7 6 5 4 3 2 1

Alice James Books are published by Alice James Poetry Cooperative, Inc.,
an affiliate of the University of Maine at Farmington.

ALICE JAMES BOOKS
238 MAIN STREET
FARMINGTON, ME 04938

www.alicejamesbooks.org

Library of Congress Cataloging-in-Publication Data

McCallum, Shara.
This strange land / Shara McCallum.
p. cm.
ISBN 978-1-882295-86-9
I. Title.
PS3563.C33446T48 2011
811'.54--dc22
2010044654

Alice James Books gratefully acknowledges support from individual donors, private foundations, the University of
Maine at Farmington and the National Endowment for the Arts. ❦

Image of Alice James used by permission of the Houghton Library, Harvard University. Call number: pf MS Am
1094, Box 3 (44d)

Cover art:

Colin Garland
"End of an Empire," 1971
Oil on canvas
120 x 90 cm
The Colin Garland Commemorative Collection
The National Gallery of Jamaica
www.natgalja.org.jm

CONTENTS

~Dear Hours~

ACKNOWLEDGMENTS

Many thanks to the editors of the following journals and anthologies, in which these poems appeared, often in earlier versions:

Antioch Review: "My Mother as Penelope" (as "Penelope"), "Ghazal"

Caribbean Review of Books: "Blue Song," "The Fall"

Connotation Press: An Online Artifact: "Miss Sally on Love"

Crab Orchard Review: "At the Hanover Museum"

Green Mountains Review: "My Mother as Persephone" (as "Persephone in Darkness"), "Domestic Interior"

Great River Review: "Penelope"

Harvard Review: "A Grammar for War"

Image: "The News"

Journal of the Motherhood Initiative for Research and Community Development: "Dear Hours"

Kestrel: "The Border"

LUNA: "The Shore," "Luck," "Parable of the Stones"

MARGIE: The American Journal of Poetry: "Diva"

Mid-American Review: "Dear History" on page 21

New England Review: "Gravid Gravitas"

Ploughshares: "History is a Room"

Prairie Schooner: "Dear History" on page 7, "Palisades" (as "Primer"), "The Pastoral Yielding to History," "Mother and Child," "Miss Sally on the Grandmother Fires"

Smartish Pace: "The Mermaid" (as "The Mother"), "A Room," "Miss Sally on Politics," "Election Days, Kingston" (as "Election Days"), "Miss Sally Explains," "Miss Sally and Fowl Run"

The Southern Review: "Psalm for Kingston"

Triquarterly: "From the Book of Mothers"

Tygerburning: "My Mother as Narcissus," "Blackberries," "October 2008"

Virginia Quarterly Review: "Couple at the Shore" (as "Under Water")
Zone 3: "Seagrape"

"Dear History" on page 24 is a revision of three separate poems, all titled "Dear History," which appeared individually in *Crab Orchard Review* and *Prairie Schooner.*

The first section of "Dear Hours" appeared as a separate poem, "For Rachel, Just before Speech," in *Image.*

"The Waves" appeared in *Evensong: Contemporary American Poems on Spirituality* (Bottom Dog Press, 2006).

"Election Days, Kingston" (as "Election Days"), "Dear History" on page 7, and "Mother and Child" also appeared in *New Caribbean Poetry: An Anthology* (Carcanet Press, UK, 2007).

"Dear History" on page 7, "Election Days, Kingston," and "At the Hanover Museum" also appeared in the online poetry anthology, *Enskyment.*

"Dear History" on page 7 and "Mother and Child" were translated into Spanish and appeared in *Poetas del Caribe Inglés: Antología,* v.2 (El perro y la rana, Venezuela, 2009).

"Dear History" on page 24 also appeared in *Review 81: Bob Marley and His Legacy* (2010).

Thank you to Bucknell University for a leave that enabled me to write some of these poems.

Above all, I am grateful to and for my husband Steven Shwartzer, who made writing this book possible, and my daughters Rachel and Naomi. Thanks always to my other family members and friends for their love and support. Deepest gratitude to Paula Closson Buck, Terrance Hayes, and Mia Leonin, for their countless readings of these poems, and to everyone at Alice James Books, particularly Mihaela Moscaliuc, Carey Salerno, and Julia Bouwsma.

For Steven, Rachel, and Naomi

Now we must bear the pieces and parts
together, as if they were the whole.

—Rainer Maria Rilke

(And when is a piece that resembles a fragment—really the whole?)

—Kimiko Hahn

PSALM FOR KINGSTON

If I forget thee, O Jerusalem
—Psalm 137

City of Jack Mandora—*mi nuh choose none*—of Anancy
        prevailing over Mongoose, Breda Rat, Puss, and Dog, Anancy
                saved by his wits in the midst of chaos and against all odds;
        of bawdy Big Boy stories told by peacock-strutting boys, *hush-hush*
but loud enough to be heard by anyone passing by the yard.

City of market women at Half-Way-Tree with baskets
        atop their heads or planted in front of their laps, squatting or standing
                with arms akimbo, *susuing* with one another, clucking
        their tongues, calling in voices of pure sugar, *come dou-dou: see*
the pretty bag I have for you, then kissing their teeth when you saunter off.

City of school children in uniforms playing dandy shandy
        and brown girl in the ring—*tra-la-la-la-la*—
                eating bun and cheese and bulla and mangoes,
        juice sticky and running down their chins, bodies arced
in laughter, mouths agape, heads thrown back.

City of old men with rheumy eyes, crouched in doorways,
        on verandahs, paring knives in hand, carving wood pipes
                or peeling sugar cane, of younger men pushing carts
        of roasted peanuts and oranges, calling out as they walk the streets
and night draws near, of coconut vendors with machetes in hand.

City where power cuts left everyone in sudden dark,
        where the kerosene lamp's blue flame wavered on kitchen walls,
                where empty bellies could not be filled,
        where *no eggs, no milk, no beef today* echoed
in shantytowns, around corners, down alleyways.

City where Marley sang, *Jah would never give the power to a baldhead*
        while the baldheads reigned, where my parents chanted
                down Babylon—*Fire! Burn! Jah! Rastafari! Selassie I!*—
        where they paid weekly dues, saving for our passages back to Africa,
while in their beds my grandparents slept fitfully, dreaming of America.

City that lives under a long-memoried sun,
        where the gunmen of my childhood have been replaced
                by dons that rule neighbourhoods as fiefdoms, where violence
        and beauty still lie down together. City of my birth—
if I forget thee, who will I be, singing the Lord's song in this strange land?

DEAR HISTORY

One's homeland is not a geographical convention,
but an insistence of memory and blood.

—Marina Tsvetaeva

DEAR HISTORY

Believe me when I tell you
I did not know her name

but remember the colour of her dress:
red, like my own school uniform.

I did not know death could come to a girl
walking home, stick in hand,

tracing circles in the dirt,
singing as she went along.

I did not know death
would find someone

for wearing the wrong colour smock
in the wrong part of town.

My parents spoke in hushed tones,
but I heard the storey of her body

dragged from street to gully,
left sullied in semen and blood.

I heard the song she sang,
the one I wish I could sing now.

Truth is, I was that girl.
Truth is, I was never there.

PALISADOES

The year the nation fell to violence,
Marley's cancer dismantled his body

and her father's schizophrenia
shook the last coins from his pockets.

The day she and her sisters left Jamaica,
their mother crept out of the house before dawn,

walking with her Twelve Tribes sistren
through the streets of Kingston to reach Bob's funeral.

In the years since, she has sifted details,
treated memory like bones to be assembled.

Did her grandmother's hands,
packing and searching for passports,

erase her mother's kisses,
placed on sleeping eyelids?

For what did the nation grieve:
Breda Bob? The dreams of a people?

Days later, her father would be dead,
found in a field, overdosed on pills.

One year after, her mother would join
them in the States. But the day

she left, how long did her grandmother pace Palisadoes
after they'd missed the first flight?

And when the plane for Miami lifted off,
were the runway lights lit up

below—a bloom of jellyfish?
Was the night overcast

so she could not see
into the darkness that surrounded them?

MISS SALLY ON POLITICS

He is a one-eye man
in a blind-eye country.

But how him can do better
when no one want to see

what going on. Every time
party man come around

him jumping up and down—
lickle puppy eager fi please.

Him tell mi is not woman
business, this election.

Is not fi mi fi understand.
Mi tell yu all the same what I know:

If yu see jack ass,
don't yu must ride it?

ELECTION DAYS, KINGSTON

There are days so long the sun
seems always overhead, a hefted
medallion hanging in the sky.
They sit in the market,
gathering like flies on fruit, linger in dust
kicked up on roads scorched by drought.
They lie on the base of the neck
like beads of sweat stalling on skin.

These are the days in a country's life
when the air is so still
it collects in folds, drapes itself
through the nostrils of young and old;
when the air is weighted with something
approximating hope.

THE WAVES

We walk into rooms that wait for us to enter them.
We walk into waves that threaten to drown us.

But they don't. They fill us instead
with salt, sand, and their own light.

As a child, from a small boat, I watched my father
swim away, ignoring my mother's pleas—her voice

sucked into the wind, my own no match
for the undertow or sharks I feared.

There are moments in a life
when everything comes apart, is ripped so clean

who you are is laid bare. My father returned to us
that day, but he was not the same man

I had seen enter those waves.

MISS SALLY EXPLAINS

What a way things come to this.
But is who we can blame
when we own picknie tek up rockstone,
licking each other down
fi prove party loyalty?
Spit in the sky, it fall in yu face.

Now we crying out fi someone
fi stop the bellyache,
begging we leaders to put an end
to bullets ricocheting off rooftops
in Back-a-Wall and Trenchtown.
People say, *Bull horn never too heavy
fi him head.* But that don't mean
yu must increase the load.

PARABLE OF THE STONES

for Mikey Smith (1954-83)

Night: the moon unhinged in its socket of light. The lane unraveled beneath
the soles of his boots.

If he had been from the wrong side of town or was humming the wrong tune,
if he had lingered too long waiting for the bus or should have steeped his tea
two minutes more before closing the front door,

if he should have said more or less of what he knew,
                              known more or less of what he did,
                                        could this night be changed?

The storey is always the same,
                      must unfold the same way:

beginning and ending
                  with the lane, the moon,
                              stones littering our path.

THE FALL

In childhood, the world was a ball she threw above her head,
watched suspended the moment before descent.

Nights from her bedroom window, she pieced together
scraps of sky between the flame tree's fringed leaves.

Sometimes in dream—or a waking dream—
she and her sisters lowered themselves over the window sill,

hoping to defy gravity's pull, a rope
tied to the bedpost and around their waists.

Did the knots hold? Now no longer sure, she knows
by day they would again wander the yard,

recording but not understanding lessons
the world revealed: *rock* and *stone*

are different words which mean the same when flung;
beauty delivers its own kind of wound.

THE PASTORAL YIELDING TO HISTORY

Sometimes the eye sees what the mind mistrusts.
Sometimes there is a green too green for belief:

sun rising over these mountains
illuminates fields unruffled by wind,

thatched hut around which foliage has grown up—
banana trees, coconut palms, and breadfruit,

broad leaves resembling hands
with fingers outstretched.

On the horizon, a man
leads a donkey across a narrow bridge.

Flanking either side of the animal, crocus bags
brim with bananas yet to ripen.

The donkey hauls freshly cut sugar cane
stacked on its back.

A cutlass dangles from the man's fingertips.
The sun is a disk boring a hole into the sky.

AT THE HANOVER MUSEUM

Lucea, Jamaica, 2000

Once many believed in a common dream
of this island, variegated skins of fruit

arrayed at market. *Every mickel mek a muckle.*
But the land keeps opening to loss—

flame tree seeds shaken loose from limbs,
sifted flour that will not rise into bread.

Stalks of cane grow, unaware of their irony,
scattered across this museum's grounds.

Inside, shackles affixed to cement blocks
have rusted to vermillion, almost beautiful.

Here, the sea breaking against cliffs
is a voice I might mistake for the past.

At the entrance to town, the sea wall stands.
Balanced on the edge of water and land,

children play in the surf. Fishermen,
visible in the distance,

will later bring in the day's catch:
snapper on a string, mackerel, even barracuda.

In a place where wind drags through leaves,
where dusk can rip daylight to shreds,

I emerge, remembering
how to eat sugar cane:

spit out the pulp,
before it grows reedy and bitter in your mouth.

MISS SALLY ON LOVE

In my time, I was a girl who like to spree.
The whole world would open fi mi

if I shift mi hips to strain
the fabric of mi skirt, just so.

Still, I did learn mi lesson
where love concern: if snake bite yu,

when yu see even lizard, crawling
with him belly on ground, yu run.

Now the gal come to mi, say she fall in love
with man who have a plan fi change.

But she nuh notice him also carry gun?
And, lawd, how she nuh see

who running the show and who
keeping house same way?

MOTHER AND CHILD

Forgive the sun for shining that day,
light glinting off the mother's nutmeg skin,
finding beauty in the most improbable places.

Forgive the child, dead in her arms,
for running into the path of a bullet
as if running after the tail of a kite.

Forgive the mother, sending him to the shop
for scallion and thyme, pressing coins
into his palm, promising sweets on return.

Forgive the ground for absorbing his blood,
for muffling footfalls of the one
who fired the gun and fled.

Forgive the mother's mouth, the wail
lodged in her throat, the groveling eyes
asking too late for someone to intervene.

Forgive the silence of the onlookers,
crowding to see. Forgive even History,
indifferent to grief.

MISS SALLY ON THE *GRANDMOTHER FIRES*

Hear what I tell yu: God promised Noah,
No more water. The fire next time.
That evening, mi sit down on the verandah
teking in a lickle fresh air when news reach
of the women dead in them sleep.
Lickle by lickle, the rest of the storey come out:
two young boys acting like men, like God himself.
153 dead—and fi what? Fi win election?

Mi dear, in all mi years I never imagine
is so low we would stoop.
For a people who know
what it is to be the lamb,
how we go lead our own
to slaughter?

DEAR HISTORY

That night in bed, I held my tongue,
listened for my words

in the sound of wind
swishing through trees.

Everything outside the window
was still and moving all at once,

so I could not tell
if silence was the sound

darkness made
fall over the earth

or if silence was within me
and I was the dark.

Earlier that day in school, teacher told us
of women set on fire,

old women, *like your grandmothers*,
killed by an unknown hand.

But they were *luminous*, I'd told myself,
the word in my mouth round and bright,

filling up the classroom,
blocking out all others.

And they were like the stars I saw at night,
on spindles of light so far from their bodies

even the heat of the flame could not make them
return to their embered skins.

BLUE SONG

In the drawing room, she surfaces: hands folded
on her lap, hair oiled and pulled into a rubber band.

Now you are presentable, her mother had said
before sending her off.

A present? Able to be present?
she wonders, fidgeting in her seat.

Her grandmother's scowl stays fixed
on her the afternoon.

Knitting needles click, keeping time
with the clock's *tick-tick-tick*.

The sun sifts through jalousies.
Dust motes drift on shafts of light.

In the garden, her father
plucks notes and chords,

and it is him she listens for
above the room's din, not music

but the sound of his fingers,
insistent on frets, twanging on strings,

the sound that will become this room,
her father, memory itself, ever-present blue song.

MISS SALLY AND FOWL RUN

Cockroach don't business in fowl run,
mi dear. How things stay,
all I after now
is a tin of bully beef, lickle eggs.
Yu see politician:
each one gwaan like him
a go change the world,
act like unoo is friend.

Mi love, only thing politician know
is how fi line him own pocket;
all of them cut
from the same piece of so-so cloth.
Once them get in, is just *kiss mi ass*
and *thank you ma'am.*

DEAR HISTORY

I could tell when my parents stopped believing.
Marcus, Marley, Manley—their gods

deserted them, leaving little
to wring between their hands.

After a time, revolution's light dims.
Ideals get exchanged for smaller needs,

milk and bread, the crumbs of peace.
In the final days, everyone tried to explain

what had gone wrong: politicians said
tourists would no longer come;

Mummy and Daddy said slavery
was the root; Granny said it was the youth,

killing each other, running wild in the streets.
The night before she and Papa moved to America,

I prayed in the dark of my room
but feared my words

could no longer spiral up to something beyond.
We will come back for you. I promise,

they'd said. When, piece by piece,
my family fled,

we didn't see the bargain
being struck: to live

in a place where memory
becomes a synonym for home.

FURY

Memory.
Which is the ghost of the body.
Or myth.
Which is the ghost of meaning.

—Eavan Boland

THE BORDER

Whatever strip of whatever border she will cross,
this girl believes in the possibility of ruin.

In a photograph taken the morning of her departure,
she stands beside a car:

the verandah's iron rails conspire with the sun,
slanting bars of light across her face;

swiveled at the waist, she twists
to catch a last glimpse of home—

or so we might imagine in order to tell this tale.
From this point forward, she will want

a dark flecked by stars and wind;
dirt roads where mermammy wanders

seeking love; a place where spider tales
are truths spun at dusk and rain hums

in the eaves, where the night's voice
is the trawling sea.

FURY

The madwoman wanders the hall of mirrors. The parrot perched on her shoulder squawks, *Again. Again,* its mantra heeded by no one. The madwoman counts minutes, sees patience as a ticking out of life's losses. In her fingers, she briefly holds each memory before letting her hands fall back at her sides. Now she is no longer a girl running in a garden saturated with lemon trees. She thinks this morning she might be the parrot mimicking language. Or perhaps she has become the single word delivered from its maw.

In the country where she lives, which is no country, the madwoman maps desire's coordinates onto her body. Each hand pressing into her back meets the others that have lingered in that spot; each lover tastes the breath of those gone before, ghosting in her kisses—the madwoman now being all women. The hysteric who cordons off danger so others can believe in safety. The anorectic who starves her flesh so others may eat. The whore whose sex blooms thorns. The mystic whose dust covered feet discredit her visions. The mother whose placid gaze masks the storm gathering fury into its centre.

MY MOTHER AS PENELOPE

Lemon rinds in the dried brook bed,
fireflies failing to light—

all, like me,
suffer the occasional drought.

Outside my window,
no islands of foliage

block my view to the shore.
No river noises trickle in.

Listen, after years of waiting,
I tire of the myth I've become.

If I am not an ocean,
I am nothing.

If I am not a world unto itself,
I need to know it.

DOMESTIC INTERIOR

The woman at the sink will always wait
for someone to enter this room.
In both hands she holds a cup, warming
her fingertips, and shifts from foot to foot.
She stares out the window and studies
the world beyond: the tree in the yard
preening itself for fall, offering a last hurrah
before winter rattles brittle limbs.
The children asleep in their cribs,
the husband busying himself with tasks—
and she, awash in late afternoon light,
dreaming herself young, remembering
his fingers on the back of her neck.
Could any touch have ever been that pure?

THE MERMAID

There is a place where the river meets the sea, where the water turns green and cold and still, a mirror in which you can see into your own eyes but nothing beneath. In Port Antonio, the children walk behind their mother, *peep-peep, cluck-cluck.*

The group descends from the house down the hill, down the winding path scattered with rocks. One of the children recognises the man who sold them bammy and fish last night for dinner and almost turns to wave, but the mother is getting farther ahead.

At the dock, surefooted, she leads the way; the children follow, stepping as if nearing the edge of a cliff. Stopping on the last wooden slat, the mother lifts her dress over her head in one swift motion. At first, the children watch in silence, then begin their protests: *No Mummy. Please don't go.*

Their voices seem to arrive from a great distance. She looks out to the island across the way, decides she will swim to it and come right back.

Through the shade of trees, patches of sunlight turn her naked body into an underwater scene. The children, howling, clench eyes shut; only the trees witness what happens next. Only they see the mother's perfect dive into the waiting depths, the sliver of water opening to take her back.

GHAZAL

Do we remember love before neglect?
For too long, mother, I've returned to your neglect.

Dusk offers a fractured memory of light.
Darkening grass conceals its own tale of neglect.

Can you teach me to remember joy?
Your life is a coupling: remorse, neglect.

By dying, my father may have been loved best.
Mother, how are we still subject to his neglect?

Bluebirds and finches return to my yard each spring.
Abandoned nests reveal the science of neglect.

Nights in bed, I've listened to my infants' cries.
Puncturing silence, that refrain: *neglect, neglect.*

In Hebrew, *Shara* means *she sings.*
What song can offer the antidote for neglect?

LUCK

Somewhere a woman with my face
sits alone in a kitchen,

leading my other life, the one
I exchanged when I entered a room

never meant for me.
Copper light saturates the window.

I sit drinking tea and you enter,
carrying spring in your arms:

bouquet of fire lilies, purple bells, white stars.
Your skin browned from sun.

A thief, I snatched this world
from my other's gaze—

round, expectant as the empty cup
in which she still swirls her spoon.

A ROOM

My mother comes in from the storm
bearing a basket of flowers,
hair wet with rain.

This morning, the storm
has moved across the island
like a woman feverishly dusting,

upending pillows, beating rugs
on her front stoop, pinning to clotheslines
laundry that will fade as it dries.

Carrying flowers, my mother offers
the simplest gesture: a gift for my father,
for this home she is trying to make.

How is a home more
than the trappings of its rooms?
Does it long to be made?

One day, in another room, a death
certificate will bear my father's name—
suicide, a word fading over time.

But in this room,
I watch my mother
come in from the storm

to stand in a door of light,
unfold flowers and lay them out to dry,
stem to stem across a table,

her hair dripping water onto wood,
marring or perfecting the task.

COUPLE AT THE SHORE

In her dreams, the sea will not let her rest,
carrying on its metronome:
rush and pull, swell and din.
The sea wants to enter this house,
finds its way inside with sand
hidden in suits, salt lingering
on skin. The woman locks doors,
latches windows, draws curtains to a close,

but its roar permeates walls.
When she wakes, she is submerged.
No dustcloths, brooms, or mops
suffice to send it out. The sea
will not let her forget
the trip and fall of his breath.

MY MOTHER AS NARCISSUS

Once I was like you, wearing solitude
as if it were a garment of the finest threads.

Mistaking loneliness for beauty, I knelt
before the pool, dipped my face toward its surface,

meeting not my reflection so much
as the stillness of its depths.

At first, it was only a test. Then each day
I had to surpass the one before,

peering longer to feel time
spinning almost to a stop.

Daughter, believe me when I tell you my flaw
was not vanity but pride. I thought

I could succeed where others had failed.
I thought I could stand to look

into the centre of myself
and not fall in.

THE SHORE

for Steve

Then, you turned from me in failing light,
trees startling into sleep,
snow rearranging itself in slender branches.

In the blue air of winter, at dusk,
I stood at the shore in icy reeds,
watching you skate a path across the pond

I was sure would crack when you reached
its centre. The clearing behind the house
opens in memory. Fear

stopped me then as now. Trying
to be brave, to get this right,
I am still the one at the water's edge,

watching the distance between us
grow wider, feeling the thread that binds us
loosen. What happens to love

in such moments? Even now,
as you sit in this morning's light
and I cannot trace the lines of your face,

I struggle to see you clearly:
not the man I love but the man
who is, finally, simply himself.

DIVA

In my twentieth year, I am a diva in training. Black, faux velvet pumps strap the instep of each foot, fasten with bright silver buckles. Black Noir mascara lengthens, thickens, and darkens my lashes, casting a spider's shadow across my powdered cheeks.

At night, in the garden outside a friend's home, the smell of gardenias twines itself into my hair. A streetlamp filters light across my body, rendering me a canvas of chalk and ash.

Later at the club, after shots of gold-flecked liqueur, we are kissing. Michael kiss-kiss-kissing me. Then Michael is kissing Mario, who calls himself Maria, whose lips flame redder than my own.

In the centre of this room, a man takes a Brillo pad to his cock. Another, on the surface of the bar, folds his torso in half, almost takes himself into his own mouth. Dancing alone, I am surrounded by bodies gilded with sweat. Between the throbbing bass, between each pulse of the strobe, in this Dry Ice filled room, I am transparent as water.

Emerging from the club near dawn, we stand on Ocean Drive, the air humid and I in nothing but bra and jeans. At twenty, I think I will change the world with lace-edged black satin. A group of boys walks by, spewing, *Puta, maricón.* Inside us, a skein of light remains unbroken and we are dancing, trying to lift ourselves out of the body's casing.

MY MOTHER AS PERSEPHONE

I painted my lips fuller, flushed
an aureole to its deepest shade,

willing him to look at me again
with the eyes of a stranger.

I lay myself across the stillness
of his frame. Even in the dark,

I could not deceive. How can we
sustain desire when the body counters

with reminders of loss?
A scar below one knee,

stretch marks, sagging flesh—
my girl, I was seduced by death,

the palimpsest
beneath skin, surfacing.

SEAGRAPE

The first night we travel to his home—
asphalt washed with rain so mist rises,

mingles with streetlamp coronas—
he points out the church he walked to and from

daily for nursery school, the hill
he rode up, delivering newspapers,

sites where I imagine him a boy
I will later love as a man, his past

spilling into our present, winters
that marked him opening again,

a procession of pond hockey games,
drifts of snow I conjure in May air.

When I try to tell him where I'm from,
I begin, *There was a place*

where each sunrise revealed the familiar
outline of the seagrape tree.

When I try to tell him who I am
I start again:

Once upon a time, there was a girl
who reached up through leaves

to pick the seagrape's fruit, and her hair
became entangled in its limbs.

BLACKBERRIES

In another life, you and I
remain the couple of our youth,

living in upstate New York,
renting a farmhouse on thirty-three acres of woods.

Walking in winter, knee-deep in snow,
we came to a clearing. I could not see

the immensity of the field for the cold.
With each inhale, air pricked my lungs,

almost erased sunlight and blackberries
we'd picked from brambles months before.

Love, marriage is that purple-black fruit,
even now searing my tongue.

PENELOPE

Long ago I was the vision you needed,
image soldered in the mind's furnace:

girl awaiting your arrival,
watching first light lacerate the sky.

You fancied the sea
a playground for your dreams,

but storms have entered you
like sound enters the skin of a drum,

changing its course.
After years adrift, you return

wanting to know how I exist
apart from you and your myths.

Husband, I learned to bear rupture
by staring down dawn,

to weave as daybreak
split open my rib cage.

Tomorrow when you leave our bed,
the sea's call already filling your ears,

you will find fishermen
hauling in nets, shimmering fistfuls

of fish with bloodied gills. Listen to me:
raise one flopping creature from the rest

to inspect the arc of its dying;
see how struggle inscribes itself on air.

Then say a prayer. Offer a blessing.
Acknowledge your power

to deliver from your palm
whatever life pulses there.

DEAR HOURS

Love set you going like a fat, gold watch.

—Sylvia Plath

GRAVID GRAVITAS

Then I came to see my body as science fiction,
imagined myself an alien sprouting wings;

craved not pickles but calamari;
devoured tart apples, lemon drops, crystallised ginger;

saw my face, as if for the first time,
reflected back to me in the toilet bowl at 6 A.M.;

suddenly noticed the nasturtium's leaves;
thought I heard grass murmuring beneath my feet;

gazed out windows as my belly rose like baking bread;
swore cinnamon scented the air I walked through;

took myself too seriously, considered myself a delicacy
smoked for days on a spit, succulent and sweet;

bumped into walls and fell down stairs
but landed, cat-like, right-side-up;

invented new words for waiting;
lingered too long on a note;

became the second hand ticking
inside each hour that moved.

DEAR HOURS

1.

We are the body moving toward demise;
we are the soul, remnant of another life.

And always, rain tapping on a zinc roof
is the sound of fingers thrumming flesh.

Always, I return
to the things of this world, tethered.

You, who have come to me
from something, somewhere, I cannot name;

you who have a voice that does not speak
any language I know yet unfurls bright wings,

alighting in each corner of this house;
you who are mine and not mine,

tell me the answers
while there is time.

2.

At Rosh Hashanah, I dip apples in honey,
bargaining for a happy New Year.

I use my teeth to separate bitter from sweet.
I chew on hope, insist its name is faith.

The weight of stones thrown into the river
to cast away sins,

this fruit in my palm whispers *ripening*
in the same breath as *ruin*.

Apple, I say to my daughter, meaning
the thing I wish to be that is not.

Apple, Apple, Apple, my one-year-old parrots,
demanding I place it on her tongue.

3.

Tired, the toddler tiptoes on padded feet.
She pitter-pats on feeted pads.

She whistles and warbles.
She burbles and bobbles.

A slug on its trail of silver,
she slooches down the hall.

A spider dangling from its last thread,
she pauses at the staircase edge.

At eighteen months, what does she know
of danger, the possible fall?

4.

Today your mouth, cheeks, the single curl
escaping your woolen hat

conjure a snapshot of me at your age:
bangled baby, head in a kerchief,

propped on a dark green lawn,
inscrutable gaze taking on the camera.

My snowflake-eating bundle of mischief
and yet-to-be-learned grief,

squealing tangle of two-year-old limbs,
spinning galaxy of self-self-self,

you totter off your sled,
only to resurface a moment later,

as if buoyed by invisible waves.

5.

From the garden, my three-year-old
plucks a zinnia,

almost snapping
the ring of petals off its stem.

At her age, in a different place,
I picked ixoras,

gathering the small blossoms,
one by one, to build a crown of flames.

If I could read my life
backward, or hers forward,

it might begin
the moment the future is written

in a child's need to possess
such a red,

or in her offering
of a flower that will not last

the hour I stand it in a vase,
propping its neck.

A GRAMMAR FOR WAR

After a day when reports of casualties
crackle out of the car radio,

pursuing me as I enter the house at dusk,
eyes wide with seeing,

ears fitted with knowledge
I know neither how to hold nor let drop,

I lay keys on the kitchen table
and scan the air wishing

again I could invent
a lexicon for grief.

If language could recover losses,
words might offer solace

the way a flock of geese follows
a preset trajectory of flight,

the way dawn's arrival restores the ginkgo's
mottled shades of green,

the way the mockingbird sings its song,
conjugating the squandered night.

THE NEWS

Nothing falls from the sky to claim me.
I am a bird with stones in its beak,
warbling an awful tune.

The news from beyond reaches me
too late. What girl has fallen now,
off what coast, into what sea?

Wasn't the water already filling with blood?
Hasn't it always been so?
These days, I close my ears

to that girl's final cries, listening
to my daughter singing at play.
Elsewhere,

a mother is facing a truth
she will have to rehearse daily to believe.
While the news clatters on,

the hem of her life will be snagged
in the moment a child
can't find her way back home.

OCTOBER 2008

Most mornings this fall I wake to rain
stitching across the lawn, crows

not yet cawing. I know dawn will collect
wayward moon, scattered stars into night's pocket.

But in the still dark, quiet room where I am,
my body forms an absence, frayed

hole in the centre of my suburban home.
Soon news will break, promising

nothing new—*endless* war, the election—
mirroring the natural world's

notion of change, leaves burning scarlet,
announcing autumn as if it were a first.

Upstairs, my husband and children
breathe into pillows their dreams.

I turn to see the woman I've become
reflected in the window's glass: a stranger

moving her finger across my cheek, trying to decode
an old storey, etched as if in Braille on my flesh.

FROM THE BOOK OF MOTHERS

The smell of your skin fades.
    I forget your heft in my arms,

your hand reaching up to cup my face
    as you nurse, curling into sleep.

Daughter, is it your aging
    or my own I fear most?

———

In fairy tales, the child is trapped
within the refrain: *motherless, motherless.*

In myth, the child is set adrift, left to water's
blind grace, the current's whims.

———

In some part of myself, I remain
    a child behind glass, watching the tall grass

through which my mother drove, the splash of blue
    drawing near. Waiting for the moment

when she decided whose life to save,
    swerving to avoid plunging into the lake.

———

If we are boats, how do we unmoor ourselves, how do we glide?

———

Instructions for a *dai* delivering a girl:

For eighty cents more,
        take the newborn child,

hold her by the waist,
        turn her upside down,

give a sharp jerk
        to snap the spinal cord.

Pronounce her
        stillborn.

———

Items for a baby girl:

Tiny bangles for each wrist.
Gold for piercing her ears at birth.

———

Dark Mother, you appear to me
as mad. Mistress of blood, death,

and the death of death,
you surface from the Ganges, pregnant,

stoop to give birth on shore,
then devour your child.

Bearer of destruction, Goddess of Time and Change,
Kali, how can I bring myself to accept your universe?

———

Motherhood: rowing away from the shore.

They say:
amniotic fluid is the ocean,

blood pumping to the mother's heart fills the child's ears with first sounds,
the infant knows her mother by smell before sight,

the cord that binds them dies once severed.
They say.

Mi navel string bury there.

When my sister's first girl came into the world,
she came with the cord wrapped around her neck.

She did not see her mother's face. She did not know
she was loved before she *was*.

Mother, I am the dark in your eye.

From my grandmother's line
eleven girls have descended, no boys

in three generations.
The women in my family repeat lives:

migrations, madness, exile,
mothers and daughters estranged—

connected by a storey
that wants to go on without end—

———

Motherhood: the doll whose head refuses to return to its body.

———

I did not hear or could not listen.
          I barely knew you when you called.

Now when it is too late
          I want to tell you I am a mother

and think I understand something
          more of grief's depths. I am a mother

like but also not like you. My friend
          (may I call you this in death?)

my child's throat I
          lean toward to kiss.

———

Motherhood: the promise of feathers against plucking fingers.

———

          I will have to admit you—unclaimed woman,
          betrayed wife, daughter of the gods, yet exiled.

          Prideful one, scorned one, vengeful one—
Medea, your daughters walk the earth, drowning

                    offspring in bathtubs and lakes,
          slashing their children's throats. Medea:

                    spectre within each of us
                    who brings forth life.

———

I recite the Hebrew alphabet each time
    I must do something my children fear.

Alef Bet Gimel Dalet...

    Voice hushed, speech slow,
        I repeat these sounds till their breathing stills,

...Lamed Mem Nun...

    tears cease, their bodies given over
        to a language we do and do not know.

———

    Motherhood: the country of want, of want, of want.

———

        The old stories had it wrong. Each woman
is within herself mother and daughter, bound

    by the same spell. The witch is also she.
So the hag. So too *Old Higue* who leaves her body

    nights to visit the child she was in the crib,
suckling the infant's blood to regain her youth,

    then burning in a brine of flesh
when she tries to return to her skin.

———

If you were a dress, I would wear you, just like my second skin.

———

Force-ripe.
Spoiled fruit.

I, Eve, in this boxcar. I, Eve, hearing the wheels
clacking on tracks, the engine's churning. I, Eve,

fitted into the other mothers.
If you see my daughters, tell them—

Final note to Demeter:

Bucket, bucket go a well.
Bucket bottom drop out.

Demeter's reply:

Bucket, bucket go a well.
Bucket bottom drop out.

Pushed from the calabash, stained by its pulp,
we were turned into little girls.

Sent to ease your life, we cooked porridge,
swept the yard, tended goats and fowl.

But the Great Spirit has taken us back,
hearing you curse us: *wutless creatures.*

Returned to oblivion, we have forgotten
the feel of your hands laying us down

by the fire. Where are you, mother,
now the spell is broken?

———

Daughter, I am the dark in your eye.

———

My two-year-old's refrain:

You tell me the answer, Mummy.

———

Dear Mother, Dear M., other, Dear other, my dear other.

———

But here you surface again,
scales glittering in the sun. With a flick of your tail,

I would follow you
to any depths. I would weave a net

from my hair, catch fish
for us to feast all day long.

I would stitch your skin with kisses,
reel in the language marooned between us.

But you will never return to me. You,
mermaid in question, of course have gone.

———

What is separation's geography?
The mother's body is the country

of our earliest memory, the soil
from which we are formed.

Our lives are an arc of flight:
away, toward, away.

———

Instructions for lighting candles for Shabbat:

Take the match to each candle's wick. With cupped palms,
pull the light toward you, encircling it with your arms.

Do this three times. Now cover your eyes
to bring the flame inside.

———

Items for mothering:

Thimble, needle, thread.
Three pinches of salt.

———

Make me remember: scallop of flesh, crescent of skin,
pulse at the base of her throat.

Help me keep the memory of my girl,
stave off her inevitable bloom.

———

Motherhood: the nitty-gritty, the dirty ditty, jingle-jangle, splash, pizzazz.

———

Sing a light song, Mummy.

Twinkle, twinkle—

No the other light song.

This little light of mine—

No. A different light song.

———

Motherhood:

———

If not the tree outside, if not the quiet within,
    if not the coming storm, if not the girl

dressing up in crinoline, the woman
    browning garlic in the pan,

if not this room, this life,
    then where, then when?

HISTORY IS A ROOM

The study of History is the study of Empire.
—Niall Ferguson

I cannot enter.

To enter that room, I would need to be a man who makes History, not a girl to whom History happened.

Mother to two daughters, I guard their lives with hope, a pinch of salt I throw over my shoulder.

To enter that room, I would need to wield a gun.

Here, I brandish weapons that serve an art my mother and grandmother knew: how to make of plantain and eggs a meal.

To enter that room, I would need to live in the past, to understand how power is amassed, eclipsing the sun.

Beneath my children's beds, I scatter grains of rice to keep duppy at bay.

To enter that room, I would need to live in the present: *This* election. *This* war.

Beneath my children's pillows, I place worry dolls to ensure their peaceful sleep.

To enter that room, I would need to bridge the distance between my door and what lies beyond.

Standing in my foyer at dusk, I ask the sea to fill the crevices of this house with its breath.

History is recounted by the dead, returned from their graves to walk in shriveled skins.

In our yard, I watch my daughters run with arms papering the wind.

History is recounted by children in nursery rhymes, beauty masking its own violence.

In my kitchen, I peel an orange, try to forget my thumb must wrest the pulp from its rind.

History is recounted in *The Book of Explanations*: AK-47 begat UZI, which begat M-16...and all the days of their lives were long.

Pausing at the sink, I think of how a pepper might be cut, blade handled so the knife becomes the fruit slit open, its seeds laid bare.

History is recounted in *The Book of Beginnings*: the storey of a people born of forgetting.

In our yard, I name the world for my children—*praying mantis, robin's egg, maple leaf*—words for lives they bring me in their palms.

To enter that room, I would need to look into the mirror of language, see in *collateral damage* the faces of the dead.

In our yard, I sow seeds, planting myself in this soil.

To enter that room, I would need to uncover the pattern of a life woven onto some master loom.

Here, I set the table, sweep the floor, make deals with the god of small things.

To enter that room, I would need to be armed with the right question: is History the start of evening or dawn returning the swallow to the sky?

Here, I light candles at nightfall, believe the match waits to be struck.

NOTE

The poems in the "Dear History" section focus on a period in my family's history and in Jamaican history from 1972 to 1981. In 1972, the year I was born, the leader of the leftist People's National Party (PNP), Michael Manley, was elected Prime Minister. Under Manley's direction, the PNP practiced "Democratic Socialism" throughout the 1970s. This, along with Manley's diplomatic ties to Cuban President Fidel Castro, led to US involvement in Jamaican politics, including CIA destabilization operations within the country. In the year leading up to the general election of 1980, it is estimated that 800 to over 1,000 people out of a population of 2.5 million were killed in election related violence. In October of 1980, Edward Seaga, leader of the conservative Jamaican Labour Party (JLP), was elected Prime Minister. On May 11, 1981, Reggae superstar Bob Marley died of cancer. His funeral, held in Jamaica ten days later, was a moment of unification for a people who had been torn apart by almost a decade of ideological and political conflict. I emigrated from Jamaica to the US on the day of Marley's funeral. My parents, both Rastafarians, were attending Marley's funeral as my younger sisters and I left the island with our maternal grandmother.

BOOK BENEFACTORS

Alice James Books and Shara McCallum wish to thank the following individuals, who generously contributed toward the publication of *This Strange Land:*

Kazim Ali

For more information about AJB's book benefactor program, contact us via phone or email, or visit us at www.alicejamesbooks.org to see a list of forthcoming titles.

Recent Titles from Alice James Books

Alice James Books has been publishing poetry since 1973 and remains one of the few presses in the country that is run collectively. The cooperative selects manuscripts for publication primarily through regional and national annual competitions. Authors who win a Kinereth Gensler Award become active members of the cooperative board and participate in the editorial decisions of the press. The press, which historically has placed an emphasis on publishing women poets, was named for Alice James, sister of William and Henry, whose fine journal and gift for writing went unrecognized during her lifetime.

Typeset and Designed Pamela A. Consolazio

Printed by Thomson-Shore
on 30% postconsumer recycled paper
processed chlorine-free